Witness History Series

BRITAIN BETWEEN THE WARS

Stewart Ross

Wayland

Titles in this series

The Arab-Israeli Conflict
Britain between the Wars
Britain since 1945
China since 1945
The Cold War
The Origins of the First World War
The Russian Revolution
South Africa since 1948
The Third Reich
Towards European Unity
The United Nations
The USA since 1945

Cover illustration: A 1935 advertisement for a Ford V-8
Saloon de Luxe.

First published in 1990 by
Wayland (Publishers) Limited
61 Western Road, Hove
East Sussex BN3 1JD, England

Series editor: Catherine Ellis
Editor: Susannah Foreman
Designer: Ross George
Consultant: Dr William Coxall, formerly senior lecturer
in Humanities at Brighton Polytechnic.

British Library Cataloguing in Publication Data
Ross, Stewart
    Britain between the wars – (Witness history series)
    1. Great Britain; 1910–1936
    I. Title   II. Series
    941.083

    ISBN 1–85210–829–0

Typeset by Kalligraphics Limited, Horley, Surrey
Printed in Italy by G. Canale & C.S.p.A., Turin
Bound in France by A.G.M.

21C

Contents

A brave new world?

ADDRESSING A gathering in Manchester in December 1918, the USA's president Woodrow Wilson declared:

> *I believe that . . . men are beginning to see, not perhaps the golden age, but an age which at any rate is brightening from decade to decade, and will lead us some time to an elevation from which we can see the things for which the heart of mankind is longing.*[1]

Woodrow Wilson was an optimist. Not everyone shared his view that the ending of the First World War marked the beginning of a new, golden era for mankind, but by and large spirits ran high now that the 'war to end all wars' was over. When the cease-fire was announced on 11 November 1918, in many towns 'the lighter-hearted part of the population ran mad' and there were 'extraordinary scenes of joviality.'[2]

The optimism and happiness shown by many at the end of 1918 was not just an expression of relief now that the fighting had stopped. The war had taught the British people what they could achieve when they pulled together, setting aside the class antagonism that had so marked the years immediately prior to 1914. Prime Minister Lloyd George promised new 'homes fit for heroes', with the co-operation of the war

Damage from a Zeppelin air raid on London, 1915. Such attacks meant that no one could avoid the scourge of war.

◀ Scenes of wild rejoicing on Armistice Day, 11 November 1918. Some people found it hard to believe that the war was really over.

▶ The British General Bruce on a tiger shoot in India, 1924. The end of the First World War meant that Britain was free to tackle the problems presented by its world-wide empire.

years carried over into the peace.

Technological advances hastened by the war, in fields such as communications and motor transport, could enrich the lives of millions. The controversial question of women's right to vote had been all but settled by a war that could not have been won without the tireless and skilled labour of the female work-force. Women could look forward to an era of unprecedented equality. Britain had survived the war with its empire – the largest the world had ever seen – intact, and its international reputation as a great power perhaps dented but still formidable. A new spirit of international co-operation abounded, soon to find expression in the League of Nations.

Yet others viewed the future with apprehension. A war that had claimed the lives of a million soldiers from Britain and its empire had shattered Victorian confidence and certainty for ever. There was a spirit of revenge abroad, as well as a desire to take up old battles where they had been dropped in 1914. The questions of Irish independence, the rights of the subject peoples of the empire, and the appalling standard of living of the urban working class had all been only shelved, not solved, during the First World War.

Perhaps, in the laughter of the dancing crowds on Armistice Day, there was as much anxiety about the future as relief at the ending of military hostilities.

1
PARLIAMENTS AND PARTIES
Domestic politics 1918–39

IN DECEMBER 1916 the Liberal politician David Lloyd George had become prime minister and leader of the small war cabinet. At the end of the war, he called a general election in December 1918. With the slogan 'a country fit for heroes to live in', Lloyd George campaigned successfully for the return of his coalition government, which remained in power until 1922. But the cabinet had the huge problems of peace-making abroad and the troubles in Ireland to deal with, as well as trying to get Britain back on its feet again. Although brilliant, Lloyd George was not generally trusted, and the country was suspicious of the ability of many MPs to understand the needs of the ordinary people. The Conservative leader Baldwin described his colleagues as 'hard-faced men who had done well out of the war'.[3] What do you think he meant by this? When an election was announced in 1922, the Conservatives broke with the coalition government and Lloyd George resigned, never again to return to office.

The fall of Lloyd George brought turmoil to British politics. With the Liberal Party in disarray, Labour, who won 142 seats in the 1922 election to the Liberals' 116, now became the second largest party in the House of Commons. Bonar Law was Tory prime minister until ill health forced him to hand over to Stanley Baldwin in 1923. At the end of the year Baldwin called an election on the question of Protection (protecting domestic industry from foreign imports, by imposing high tariffs on imports), the result of which was a hung parliament, defeat for the Conservatives, and Britain's first Labour government under Ramsay MacDonald. Without a majority in the House of Commons, however, Labour could do little more than struggle on to the end of 1924, when they were soundly defeated in another general election by a Conservative Party which had now renounced Protection.

Among the better-off classes there was a mood of irresponsible pleasure-seeking in the 1920s. 'Bright Young Things' are here shown dancing late into the night at a London hotel.

◀ What do you think these poorly-paid industrial workers thought of the extravagance enjoyed by the dancers in the picture opposite?

▼ An election poster put out in 1931 by the coalition National Government. It suggests that only they can deal with the problem of unemployment.

Baldwin's steady leadership enabled his government to survive the General Strike in 1926 (see page 27) and remain in power until the 1929 general election. With 288 seats to the Conservatives' 260 (the Liberals won only 59), Labour now formed their second government. But their administration soon ran into serious trouble as a world-wide economic slump followed the crash on the New York stock market in October 1929. Unemployment soared to over 20 per cent of the work-force. In the face of this crisis, in 1931 MacDonald called for Conservatives and Liberals to join him in a National Government. This split the Labour Party.

Backed by 521 MPs in the Commons, the National Government under MacDonald (1931–5), Baldwin (1935–7) and Neville Chamberlain (1937–40), remained in power until the Second World War (1939–45). Particularly after the 1935 election, it became increasingly a Conservative administration under another name. The Government had little conspicuous success in dealing with the country's economic problems, but with the rise of the Nazi Party in Germany in the 1930s it became preoccupied with foreign affairs and rearmament.

The Conservatives

The Conservatives were undoubtedly the most successful of the three major British political parties in the inter-war years. The table below illustrates their success in the general elections between 1918 and 1935:

Year	No. of Conservative seats (total seats in brackets)	% of electorate voting Conservative
1918	335 (707)	32.6
1922	345 (615)	38.2
1923	258 (615)	38.1
1924	419 (615)	48.3
1929	260 (615)	38.2
1931	473 (615)	55.2
1935	432 (615)	53.7

At every single election the Conservatives won a higher share of the vote than any other single party, and only in 1929 did they fail to win more seats. Only when Labour were in power in 1924 and 1929–31 were Conservatives out of office. Two further minor points are worth mentioning: in 1918 the Conservatives were officially entitled the Conservative and Unionist Party, signifying their commitment to preserving the union of Ireland with the rest of the British Isles; secondly, the figures above for 1935 include forty-five Labour and Liberal MPs who supported the National Government.

Why do you think the Conservatives were so successful during this period? For much of the inter-war period, opposition to the Conservatives was divided between Liberal and Labour parties, both of which stood for a more radical approach to the country's problems. But they undermined each other, as in 1922 when Labour won 142 seats, and the Liberals 116. During this period both the Liberal and Labour Parties became seriously divided. The Liberals split in 1916 when Lloyd George replaced Asquith as prime minister; Labour divided in 1931 between those who supported MacDonald in his National Government, and those who

Stanley Baldwin, the Conservative leader for much of the inter-war period. What sort of image do you think he hoped to create by smoking a pipe?

Chamberlain, French prime minister Daladier, Hitler and Mussolini at the Munich peace conference, 1938. After the meeting Chamberlain said that he brought 'Peace in our time'.

followed an independent Labour line. Could the Conservatives' success be based simply on the weakness of their opponents?

Conservative beliefs were based on two qualities, flexibility and moderation. For example, after 1921 they dropped the policy of union with Ireland which before the war had been a cornerstone of their party. Conservative flexibility is shown particularly in their attitude towards Protectionism (see page 6). They adopted it in 1923, dropped it soon afterwards, only to take it up again in the National Government in 1932. If electoral success, and the nation's needs, seemed to demand a change of policy, then the Conservatives were prepared to make it. Was such an attitude just a cynical quest for power, or realistic, practical politics?

'I am opposed to Socialism,' said Stanley Baldwin, 'but I have always endeavoured to make the Conservative Party face left in its anti-Socialism'.[4] What do you think he meant by 'face left'? Can you find the same moderate attitude in this extract from a book by the Conservative Harold Macmillan, written in 1938, entitled *The Middle Way*?

> . . . it is impossible to regard the real issue of today as being that of a struggle between the theories of free competition and planned production . . . the two systems have in practice merged.[5]

Labour

The Labour Party was born with the formation of the Labour Representation Committee in 1900, although its roots went back to the Fabian Society of the nineteenth century. In 1918, when there were sixty-three Labour MPs in the House of Commons, it adopted a new Socialist Constitution. This promised widespread social reform, a redistribution of the country's wealth from the richer to the poorer classes, and state ownership of major industries. In 1917 the communists had seized power in Russia through revolution, causing many of the more conservative and better-off British citizens to fear that a similar event might take place in Britain. The cartoon below appeared in *Punch* in October 1924, at the time of the General Election. What does the shaggy figure represent? Do you consider this cartoon a fair electioneering tactic?

Nevertheless, by 1922 Labour was the second largest party in the Commons. The next year, with the support of 191 MPs (compared with the Conservatives 258 and 159 Liberals) and the votes of almost 4½ million people, they formed their first government. However, Labour did not have overall control of the House of Commons. As was pointed out at the time, they enjoyed office but not power. The majority of the cabinet

A 1924 *Punch* cartoon, portraying Labour voters as communist supporters.

ON THE LOAN TRAIL.

were of working-class origin. What do you think the historian A.J.P. Taylor meant when he described this as:

a real social revolution . . . the great public schools and the old universities eclipsed for the first time.[6]

But there was no political revolution from either of the two inter-war Labour governments (1924 and 1929–31). The socialist intellectual, Beatrice Webb, believed that Labour were being given:

. . . a chance of playing the game of government under conditions in which they can be controlled by the general will of the whole community . . . its leaders will become educated in the realities of political life and in the work of administration; and even their future behaviour as His Majesty's Opposition will become more responsible, more intelligently courteous and bold.[7]

Unable to pass major reforms, to some extent the first two Labour governments were primarily concerned with demonstrating that they were not revolutionaries, but respectable parliamentary democrats. However, in several large towns and cities where Labour won control of local councils, they were able to begin widespread programmes of reform in matters such as housing.

Any chance Labour might have had of putting their socialist principles into practice was ruined by the effects of the economic crisis which overtook the nation at the end of 1929. Unemployment soared, tax revenue fell, exports collapsed. When the prime minister announced his National Government in 1931, only four Labour ministers and eight backbenchers followed him. Gaining 52 seats in the election of 1931 and 154 in 1935, Labour remained a party of opposition, biding its time.

▲ Ramsay MacDonald, Labour's first prime minister.

◀ Between the wars Britain's armed forces were run down. This battle cruiser was sold in 1921.

Decline of the Liberal Party

In the general election of January 1906 the Liberal Party attracted 2,757,883 votes (49 per cent of the total vote) and won 400 out of the 670 seats in the House of Commons. In 1918, twelve years later, they could muster the support of only a quarter of the vote, divided between the 133 Coalition Liberals and the 28 Liberals who would not follow Lloyd George. From that date onwards party support fell steadily away, while that of the Labour Party rose. In 1935 only twenty-one independent Liberal MPs were returned, supported by a meagre 6.4 per cent of the vote.

Three strands can be separated in the spectacular collapse of Liberalism:

1 There was personal hostility between Asquith, Liberal prime minister from 1908 to 1916, and Lloyd George, prime minister from 1916 to 1922. By late 1916 it was clear that Asquith did not have the energy or skills necessary for a successful war leader. Lloyd George was the obvious man to replace him, but although very able, he often inspired mistrust in those with whom he worked: people called him 'the Welsh Wizard'. When he became prime minister, a number of Liberals remained loyal to Asquith, thus dividing their party.

2 The reorganization and reform of the Conservative and Labour parties. Before the First World War the Conservatives had

The Liberal prime minister H. H. Asquith, who led into the First World War a party that had been pledged to peace.

One of the outstanding British politicians of the twentieth century, David Lloyd George. When he became prime minister in 1916, some Liberals remained loyal to his predecessor, Asquith, thus splitting their party.

acquired a rather negative reputation, opposing most change and social reform. During the inter-war years, under the careful and astute leadership of Baldwin, they came to be seen as a more moderate party, capable of reasoned reforms such as the 1936 Education Act (proposing a school leaving age of fifteen) and the 1937 Factory Act (further limiting the working hours of women and young people, and establishing improved working conditions), but at the same time they kept their image of being thoroughly reliable and trustworthy.

From 1918–39 Labour also changed. The electorate now saw them as the party of reform, whose ideas could herald a more just society. Party organization was tightened, and the moderation of the two Labour governments quieted people's fears that the party was bent solely on destruction.

3 The Liberals found themselves stuck between the Conservative and Labour parties.

The crucial time of change was the First World War, with its international military conflict, necessary restrictions on personal freedoms (such as conscription and censorship), and its shelving of all plans for social reform. How could the Liberals, the party of peace, liberty and reform, justify taking Britain into such a war? And by 1918 the world had changed.

As T. Wilson, the historian of Liberal decline, has written:

> *During the inter-war years it was fashionable to classify the Liberals as a 'capitalist' party, which had involved Britain in an 'imperialist' war, and was incapable of . . . speaking for the workers.*[8]

The Liberal Party has been described as having been left behind by the tide of history. Do you think this is a fair assessment?

2

POVERTY AMID PLENTY
The British economy 1918–39

THE FIRST WORLD WAR imposed enormous strains on the British economy. It stimulated heavy industries, such as shipbuilding and engineering, which in turn helped the basic production of coal, iron and steel. Millions of workers, particularly women, were found employment, who would not otherwise have done so. At the same time thousands of skilled managers and labourers were killed in the fighting. The government borrowed huge sums of money from abroad, which left the nation in debt. By 1919, £800 million was owed to the USA. With trade and communications disrupted by the fighting, and the nation's resources concentrated at home, overseas markets for British goods and services had been lost.

It is not surprising, therefore, that following a short boom which had fallen off by the end of 1920, after the war the British economy entered a long period of difficult readjustment. The story of what happened is best told in figures.

Look carefully at the following table of prices and real wages. Real wages reflect what people can buy with their earnings. Do the figures suggest that people were better or worse off during this period?

Date	Prices of consumer goods raw materials and food (1866–77 = 100)	Real wages per annum (1930 = 100)
1920	251	91.2
1925	136	91.7
1930	97	100.0
1935	84	108.3

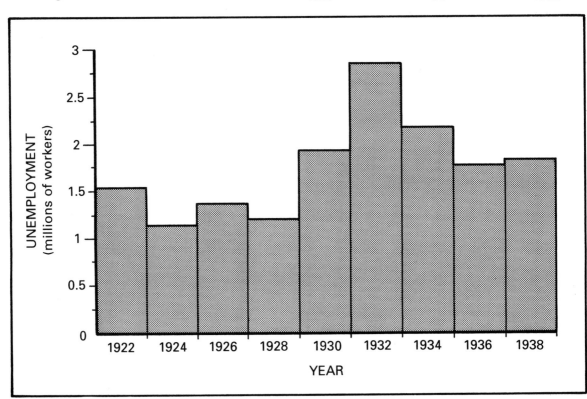

◄ An early assembly line for Morris cars, 1930. How does it differ from a modern car assembly plant?

▼ A British-made railway engine being loaded on to a ship at Liverpool for export. Such manufactures were badly hit by the world slump of 1929.

As prices fell, so the spending power of wages rose, making wage-earners better off.

Now consider these figures for the output of Britain's traditional major industries:

Date	Shipping completed (1,000s of tonnes)	Coal production (millions of tonnes)
1920	2,440	233.2
1925	813	247.1
1930	965	247.8
1935	690	225.8

Date	Steel production (1,000s of tonnes)	Cotton exports (millions of metres)	
1920	9,145	1920–29	3,874
1930	7,112	1930–39	1,801

Britain's import/export figures and balance of payments make similarly gloomy reading:

Date	Imports (millions of £s)	Exports (millions of £s)	Balance of payments (millions of £s)	
1920–29	1,259.2	791.4	1920–24	161
1930–39	841.0	438.9	1925–9	83
			1930–34	−27
			1935–8	−24

How can an economy support falling production and higher real earnings? The answer is made alarmingly clear in the graph opposite, which demonstrates the central problem of the inter-war economy.

During all the inter-war years at least ten per cent of the British work-force were unemployed. In 1932 the figure had risen to 23 per cent: almost a quarter of those who wanted work could not find it. In some areas, particularly those that had been based around traditional industries, the figures were far worse. For example, in 1933 the unemployment rate in Jarrow in the north of England stood at 80 per cent. In 1936 this resulted in the Jarrow march, a peaceful demonstration against unemployment, when desperate workers marched from Jarrow to London.

Why was the overall picture of the British economy between the wars one of contrasts? On the one hand, old industries were in decline, producing deep, depressing pockets of unemployment. On the other, for those in work, these were years of prosperity and a rising standard of living.

Depression

A modern historian has recently written of the economic situation in Britain during the inter-war years:

> *. . . the dominating impression of the era is one of economic dislocation and instability . . . world war[s] and a severe and persistent depression marked one of the most chequered periods for economic life both at national and local levels. The consequences of these events were obvious enough in the losses, upheaval and devastation caused by the wars and in the lengthening dole queues and derelict communities of the depressed areas.*[10]

The key word here is 'impression', for, as we have seen on page 4, the position was not wholly bleak. So what has created our lop-sided view?

The spectacular collapse of the New York stock market in October 1929, known as the 'Wall Street Crash', with the subsequent international industrial and trade depression, captured the imagination of the world, particularly when wealthy American stockbrokers, reduced to poverty almost overnight, sought escape through suicide.

The table below highlights the regional nature of Britain's unemployment. Why do you think certain areas were so seriously depressed?

Region	% of unemployed, out of work for 12 months or more[11]
South East	6
South West	12
North West	23
Wales	37

Anxious investors block Wall Street in New York as they await news of their fate at the time of the great crash in share prices, 1929.

An unemployed man on a street corner in Wigan, 1939. This famous photograph is usually entitled 'Despair'. What do the man's shoes tell you about his condition?

The plight of the stricken families received widespread and shocking coverage from writers and photographers.

> *It got you slowly, with the slippered stealth of an unsuspected, malignant disease.*
>
> *You fell into the habit of slouching, of putting your hands into your pockets and keeping them there; of glancing at people, furtively, ashamed of your secret, until you fancied that everybody eyed you with suspicion . . .*
>
> *Nothing to do with time; nothing to spend; nothing to do tomorrow nor the day after; nothing to wear; can't get married. A living corpse; a unit of the spectral army of three million lost men.*[12]

Unemployment was something which governments seemed unable to do much about. We now know that the sort of slump which afflicted Britain between the wars could probably have been dealt with by government spending on public works and other projects. Many economists, including J.M. Keynes, were suggesting this as a solution to the lack of money supply at the time.

Yet most politicians, even those in the National Government, believed that it was their duty to keep a balanced budget and low prices. They believed that by these methods the economy could recover on its own accord from what they saw as merely a cyclical depression. Do you think they were justified in their beliefs?

Prosperity

The historian A.J.P. Taylor entitled the period from 1925 to 1929 'The Years of Gold'.[13] He was not just referring to the fact that this was a time when the pound sterling was on the 'gold standard' – that is, the currency could be freely exchanged at the bank for gold or silver:

> *The last years of the nineteen-twenties . . . were a good time, or, at any rate, a breathing space between two times of trouble.*[14]

Others have extended Taylor's idea of a 'breathing space' to the whole of the inter-war period. Consider the title of one of the best-known books on this era, *The Long Week-end*, by Robert Graves and Alan Hodge; or this poem by Louis MacNiece published in the *New Statesman* in 1940:

> Twenty years forgetting
> Twenty years turning the Nelson eye
> Our wings heavy with the pollen
> of flowers about to die
> We said, 'Make merry in the sunshine',
> At least we are alive.[15]

The 'Nelson eye' suggests that people didn't look at what they didn't want to see. What do you suppose this was? 'Wings heavy with pollen' gives the impression that there were riches abounding in a society which

A 1927 advertisement for a new luxury car. Was it wrong that the wealthy could afford expensive new cars at a time when the unemployed had only just enough money for food?

THE SAVING OF LABOUR.

The Robot. "MASTER, I CAN DO THE WORK OF FIFTY MEN."
Employer. "YES, I KNOW THAT, BUT WHO IS TO SUPPORT THE FIFTY MEN?"

This *Punch* cartoon of 1933 illustrates the problems an employer faced when he bought machinery to make his factory more efficient.

was intent on enjoying itself. For those in work this was very probably so:

In spite of the problems of the traditional sectors, the inter-war years were marked by substantial economic growth, representing a significant improvement on the Edwardian era and in comparison with most other European countries.[16]

New industries blossomed. Among the leaders were electricity (by 1938, 2 in 3 houses were wired for electricity, compared with 1 in 17 in 1920), motor-vehicle manufacture (507,700 cars a year by 1937) and plastics.[17] By the later 1930s, the building and

armaments industries were booming too. Retail chain stores flourished, as did the practices of hire-purchase and advertising. As average living standards rose, the modern consumer society came into being.

These figures for average annual earnings tell of the effect of rising production on those able to benefit from it:

Employment Earnings in £s[18]	1924	1935
Pottery workers	171	173
London bus and train drivers	190	218
Fitters	157	212
Coalface workers	180	149
Bank clerks	280	368
Doctors	(1922–4) 756	(1935–7) 1,094

Which group of workers of those listed above fared worst between 1924 and 1935? Do you think that the cartoon on the left helps to explain why the less skilled workers were finding it difficult to benefit from the new economic prosperity?

An early Hurricane fighter plane. Government spending on armaments in the late 1930s helped to lift the economy out of depression.

A shrinking world

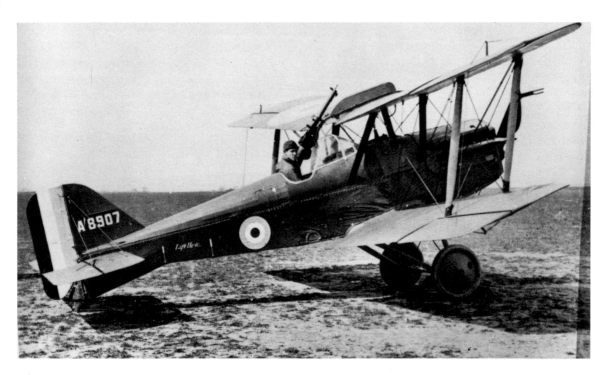

One of the unforeseen effects of the First World War was an acceleration of technological development. This was marked in the field of communications and transport, particularly aviation.

It was only in 1909 that the Frenchman, Louis Blériot, had flown his crude monoplane from France to England, so piloting the first aircraft over the Channel. Ten years later the RAF pilots Captain Alcock and Lieutenant Brown, in their twin-engined Vickers-Vimy bomber, became the first to fly the Atlantic in a heavier-than-air machine. By the 1930s, air travel, whether by plane or airship, had become commonplace, if still too expensive to be popular. When Chamberlain went to meet Adolf Hitler at Munich in 1938, for speed and convenience he chose to make the journey by plane. And when war broke out in 1939 it was the bombers' aerial attack, not invasion, which filled most British inhabitants with the greatest dread. The two pictures above and right show quite clearly how aircraft developed between the wars.

A First World War SE5 fighter, slow and armed only with a single machine gun.

The expansion of the motor vehicle industry was perhaps technologically not so dramatic: the real change here was mass production. Assembly line production of cars began in the USA in 1913. Soon, small and cheap Austins and Morrises were pouring from British factories. Vehicle output rose to over 300,000 a year by 1939, by which time there were over 3 million vehicles on the road, compared with less than 150,000 in 1910.[19] An Austin Seven could be bought for about £100 – by looking at the earnings chart on page 19 you can work out what proportion of a person's income would be needed to buy one.

With the development of motoring, roads had to be considerably improved, the first dual-carriageways being built in the 1930s. Nevertheless, many roads remained inadequate, making motoring in vehicles that were built with little attention to passenger safety an extremely dangerous occupation compared with today. Motor racing claimed scores of victims every year. Traffic jams became common as the motor coach, bus and private car attracted passengers away from the already struggling railway system.

The other area of communication which developed rapidly at this time was the transmission of the spoken word. Private telephones were unusual outside the homes of the upper and middle classes, but by 1939 there was hardly a household without a wireless (radio). The British Broadcasting Company (BBC) was formed in 1922, becoming a public corporation under its Director-General, John Reith, in 1926.

Serious, independent, educational and determined to uphold what it saw as the highest moral and artistic standards, the BBC played a major part in moulding the taste and even the spoken accents of the nation. Although stuffy – forbidding any form of swearing or even music that might be considered degenerate – the BBC helped to hold the nation together during the difficult years of depression.

▲ The first Supermarine Spitfire, 1936. It was several times faster and more heavily armed than the biplane in the picture opposite, which was built about twenty years before it.

◄ An early Austin 7. This cheap car brought motoring within the price range of many middle-class families.

3
THE PEOPLE OF BRITAIN
A divided nation

BY 1919 BRITAIN was an urban society. About 80 per cent of its population, which rose from 42.8 million in 1921 to 46.9 million by 1939, lived in towns and cities. The increase in population was accounted for by better medical care (there were 50 per cent more doctors in 1939 than in 1919) rather than by an increase in the birth-rate. The average number of children born to a couple marrying in the first decade of the century was 3.4; by 1940 this figure had fallen to 2.[20]

The country was still dominated by an élite of wealthy men who had benefited from public school and Oxford or Cambridge educations. In 1936–8, 1 per cent of all individuals owned 55 per cent of the nation's wealth (60 per cent from 1924–30), while three-quarters of the population could have sold all they possessed for less than £100.[21] 'Exaggerated class distinctions have been diminishing over a period of about thirty years,' wrote George Orwell in 1943–4:

> . . . but newcomers to England are still astonished and sometimes horrified by the blatant differences between class and class. The majority of the people can still be 'placed' in an instant by their manners, clothes, and general appearance . . . But the most striking difference of all is in language and accent . . . And though class distinctions do not exactly coincide with economic distinctions, the contrast between wealth and poverty is very much more taken for granted than in most countries.[22]

Shooting parties were a favourite pastime among the upper classes during the 1930s.

▶ Ascot fashions, 1919. Only the very wealthy could afford such expensive elegance.

◀ If you look carefully at the doors of this railway carriage you will see that even for travel the social classes were kept apart – although this group of schoolboys appears to be breaking the rules!

Most observers agree with what Orwell has to say about the English class system between the wars, although they would point out that it applied not only to England but to the whole of the United Kingdom. Can you identify the features that Orwell suggests divided one class from another? They seem to be wealth, behaviour, appearance and language. Social historians would add further criteria, such as education, employment and housing. Do you think that these differences still apply today?

There are, however, problems in trying to define a class system too tightly. It is generally accepted that there were an upper, middle and working class in Britain between

the wars, with most people categorized into the last group. But there were no clear boundaries between the classes, and within each one there was a whole range of subtle gradations. A doctor and a bank clerk, for example, would both be considered middle class, but the social and economic differences between them were marked.

Moreover, as Orwell noticed, the country was changing. There was increasing social mobility, as men and women either improved their lot, or fell on hard times. Ramsay MacDonald, twice prime minister, was born into poverty in the Scottish fishing village of Lossiemouth. His example gave some hope to the depressed millions.

The working classes

Membership of the working class was primarily defined by the nature of a person's work, or lack of it. At the very bottom of the social scale were the tramps and vagabonds, travelling round the country, staying in shelters or 'spikes' as they were known. You will find a moving description of their wretched lives in George Orwell's *Down and Out in Paris and London*.

Scarcely better off were the millions of unemployed and their families. As late as 1939 almost a quarter of these had been out of work for over a year.[23] Life for the unwaged was indescribably hard, as this report from a health visitor shows:

Mrs. J's husband's been out of work 14 weeks and there's five of them starving on 15s [75p] a week . . . Mrs. J., a young woman of 26 had, as the neighbours said, 'gone away almost to a skeleton' through sheer starvation. Though she was nursing her baby, I found that all the food she herself had had yesterday was a cup of tea at breakfast-time, and tea and two slices of bread and butter, provided by a married sister living near, at tea-time . . . From the husband's unemployment pay of £1, 5s [25p] a week had to go to pay off a debt, 6s 3d [31p] for rent, and only 8s 9d [44p] was left for food and fire. A school dinner for the eldest child was divided with his four-year-old brother every day and saved them from utter starvation.[24]

A row of terraced houses beside a cobbled street in Leicester, 1933. The house nearest the camera is for sale – what class of person could afford to buy it?

It would be wrong to imagine that this was typical of all working-class life. For the skilled or semi-skilled workers in the

◀ London slums in 1922. Were these the 'homes fit for heroes' that Lloyd George had promised at the end of the war?

▶ Unemployed men hearing that the government had just cut the 'dole' by 10 per cent in September 1931. Why do you think that the audience did not turn violent?

Midlands or the south of the country, there was a definite improvement in living standards during the inter-war period, particularly in households where there was more than one wage earner. Extra money was spent on clothes, food, a radio, visits to the cinema, pub or races, and even on vacations by the sea. It was still unheard of for working-class people to holiday abroad. Why do you think this was?

Most working-class housing was small and old. On the left is an example of typical terraced houses. For poorer people, bath-rooms were still not commonplace, nor were indoor toilets. Lighting was frequently by gas or oil lamp, while coal or wood fires provided for cooking and heating. In 1947, almost 70 per cent of all houses in Britain had been built before 1919.[25] Nevertheless, the government did encourage slum clearance, especially in the 1930s: between April 1934 and March 1939, 245,272 unsatisfactory houses were pulled down or closed, leading to the rehousing of 1,001,417 people.[26] But members of the working class could hardly ever consider buying their own homes.

Trade unions

Modern British trade unionism was born in the last quarter of the nineteenth century. As the legal restrictions on union activity were gradually withdrawn, so the working classes, whose labour had previously been shamefully exploited, rapidly learned to group together to demand improvements in pay, hours and conditions of work. Their chief weapon was the withdrawal of their labour: the strike.

Before the First World War the number of working days lost through strike action rose from 1.5 million in 1904 to 10.2 million in 1911, and 40.8 million in 1912.[27] Much of the story of British trade unionism in the next 27 years is told in the table below. The left-hand column shows an overall decline in the number of trade unions, while the next column indicates that trade union membership fluctuated, but not in proportion to the number of unions. What does this suggest about the changes in size of individual trade unions? In 1920 nine small unions combined to form the Amalgamated Engineering Union. Would a larger union with a widespread membership have more influence than a smaller one?

Commuters travelling to work in their private cars during the General Strike of 1926. The strike, the only one of its kind ever called in Britain, lasted eight days.

Year	No. of trade unions	No. of trade-union members (in millions)	No. of trade-union members affiliated to T.U.C.* (in millions)	No. of working days lost in strikes during the year (in millions)[28]
1914	1,260	4.1	2.7	9.9
1916	1,225	4.6	3.1	2.45
1918	1,264	6.5	5.3	5.9
1920	1,384	8.3	6.4	26.6
1922	1,232	5.6	4.4	19.85
1924	1,194	5.5	4.35	8.4
1926	1,164	5.2	4.2	162.2
1928	1,142	4.8	3.7	1.4
1930	1,121	4.8	3.7	4.4
1932	1,081	4.4	3.4	6.5
1934	1,063	4.6	3.4	0.96
1936	1,036	5.3	4.0	1.8
1938	1,024	6.0	4.7	1.3

* The TUC is the Trades Union Congress, the national federation of trade unions. It has close links with the Labour Party.

Study of the right-hand column suggests various points about trade unionism during this period. In view of what was happening to the British economy (see pages 14–15) why was it that in periods of prosperity workers were more inclined to join a union and take strike action than during years of slump, when unemployment was high?

Two further points need to be born in mind. First, trade union membership never accounted for more than about 45 per cent of the work-force; and, second, trade unionism was essentially working-class and male. Female and 'white-collar' workers were reluctant to unionize.

The General Strike occurred between 4 May and 12 May 1926. The TUC called out all workers in support of the coal miners, who were being asked to accept longer hours of work for lower wages. Baldwin's government recruited Special Constables, used troops and volunteers to keep essential services going and controlled all the information networks (such as the press). The strike collapsed after eight days, although the miners, who felt betrayed, remained out until August.

The cartoon below appeared in the popular newspaper the *Daily Express* on 19 May 1926. The triumphant British lion is back at its desk. What does this suggest might have been the attitude of a large number of British people to the strike?

A *Daily Express* cartoon published shortly after the collapse of the General Strike, 1926. Which side in the dispute do you think the paper supported?

BUSINESS AS USUAL.
"NOW WHERE WERE WE, MISS, WHEN THAT FELLOW INTERRUPTED US?"

Women

SHADE OF OLD MILITANT : "So this is what I fought for!"

A cartoon of 1927 suggesting that women did not have to be unattractive to be emancipated. Can you identify the man at the door of number 10 and the ghostly figure with the battle-axe? Is it significant that the young woman is shown to be smoking?

The story of the rights of women is a long and uneven one. Between the wars many important advances were made towards the position where women could enjoy economic, political, and social equality with men; but still, as one historian comments:

> Many of the high hopes of the early feminist pioneers for full equality had not been achieved. Equal pay and equal opportunities were still more talked about than practised and women had still to go a very long way before sloughing off the traditional roles and attributes assigned to them by men and willingly, in most cases, accepted by women.[29]

Do the pictures opposite indicate that the degree of freedom afforded to women depended on their social and economic class? Perhaps the cartoon above reinforces this idea?

There were essentially four forces tending to greater equality for women.

1 Legislation. Here are the main Acts of Parliament of the inter-war years that helped women:

1918 Representation of the People Act entitled women over thirty who were householders or married to householders to vote, and to become MPs. Countess Markiewicz was the first woman to be elected to Parliament.

1919 Sex Disqualification (Removal) Act opened up most professions to women. Nancy Astor became the first woman to take a seat in Parliament.

1923 Matrimonial Causes Act made divorce easier for women, who could also deny unsuitable ex-husbands access to the children.

1924 Guardianship of Infants Act made husband and wife joint guardians of children.

1925 Married Women's Property Act enabled married women to keep control of their own property.

1927 Divorce made easier to obtain.

1928 Representation of the People Act gave women the vote on equal terms to men.

1935 New English Law of Property enabled married women to dispose of their property as they wished.

1937 Divorce permitted for insanity and desertion.

▼What signs are there in this photograph, which was taken in 1925, that the two women are determined to be treated on an equal footing with men?

▲ Women shelling peas in 1924. The work was dull, and very badly paid – why were women doing it?

2 Employment. Helped by the country's need for their labour during the First World War, more women could now find financial independence through earning their own income. However, married women were still expected to stay at home, and women's wages were generally considerably lower than men's.

3 Birth-control. Between the wars, healthy and reliable means of birth-control (used by 66 per cent of women married between 1935 and 1939) meant that, for the first time, the majority of married women were freed from the drudgery of endless child rearing.[30]

4 A change in thinking. Influenced by modern writers, such as the novelist D. H. Lawrence, there was a gradual advance in the belief that women had physical, social and psychological needs and rights just as men had; men and women might be different, but they were equal.

The middle classes

A typical scene from British middle-class life in the 1930s. Husband and wife are lovingly attending to their car, which is proudly parked outside their respectable suburban home.

In the latter half of the twentieth century the great majority of British people regard themselves as middle class. This was not so between the wars. In 1931, over 70 per cent of those in employment were engaged in manual labour, about 7 per cent belonged to the upper classes of employers and proprietors, leaving about 23 per cent as 'white-collar workers' – the middle classes.

Within this class there were a number of gradations, as this table shows:

	% of working population[31]
Managers and administrators	3.7
Higher professionals and technicians	1.1
Lower professionals and technicians	3.5
Foremen and inspectors	1.5
Clerks	6.7
Salesmen and shop assistants	6.5

At the top end of this scale were barristers and businessmen, earning perhaps over £10,000 a year, a considerable sum. (Anyone with more than £1,000 p.a. was very comfortably off.) At the lower end, a shop assistant might earn as little as £150 a year, less than a skilled labourer. So membership of the middle class was not just a matter of income, but of other, more subtle, differences.

The middle classes were concerned with the impression they created; above all they sought respectability. The virtues they applauded were sobriety, diligence, perseverance and dependability, for these qualities enabled them to keep up appearances:

Men drawing comfortable salaries were soon tempted to acquire not only their jerry-built villas, but cheap cars, wireless sets, furniture and other amenities, on the 'never-never' [hire purchase] system. With each new obligation they became more and more the slaves of their employers . . . Mr. Smith may have been a hero at home, but he became a terrified rabbit when he thought of [losing] his 'little palace' at Colindale, his Kozy Kot at Wembley, or his overdue payment on his Austin Seven.[32]

Increasing numbers of middle-class families owned their own suburban homes: 2½ million houses were built for private ownership between the wars; many, like those in the picture on the facing page, were semi-detached, costing about £450, and requiring only a £25 deposit. Their salary-earning owners strove to speak 'properly' (that is, with BBC accents), always dressed neatly and invariably employed someone to help run the home. As family size fell, so there was more money for spending on new gadgets such as electric cookers, irons and vacuum cleaners, while children received more attention.

An early washing machine. Inventions such as this did away with the need for servants, but this was counterbalanced by the fact that they created work in the factories that made the new gadgets.

The wealthy

From the Restoration of Charles II in 1660 to the sweeping social and economic changes in the twenty-five years that followed the Second World War, power in Britain rested largely with a privileged, wealthy élite. The secret of this minority's success was its flexibility, a feature almost unique among traditional European governing classes. Successful entrepreneurs and businessmen were continually absorbed into its ranks, while families unable to maintain the levels of expenditure expected of them fell away. This was just as true during the inter-war years as it had ever been.

To contemporaries, however, this process was not always apparent. 'The old order is doomed,' wrote the Duke of Marlborough.[33]

Between the wars, hunting, shooting and fly fishing – all expensive hobbies – were still regarded as activities suitable only for the better-off classes. Only they could afford to keep horses and hounds.

Writing in 1940, Robert Graves and Alan Hodge felt that after the First World War:

> *The former 'ruling class', whose sons had gone into Parliament and the services as a matter of course, was now forced more and more into business . . . 'Society' had ceased to have any strict meaning . . . it had to earn its living like any other class.*[34]

Yet the historian C.L. Mowat could write:

> *Certainly 'society' did not disappear. The* Tatler *and the* Sporting and Dramatic *[magazines of fashionable gossip] continued to feast their readers with pictures of titled men and women at meets of the Quorn or the Pytchley [fox hunts], at shooting parties, at Goodwood or Ascot, at the Eton and Harrow match, at Cannes or Biarritz.*[35]

Which of the two views outlined above do you think the following figures support?

The Duke of Windsor, who had abdicated as Edward VIII, on the day of his marriage to the American divorcee, Mrs Wallis Simpson.

- In 1922, '1 per cent of the population owned two-thirds of the national wealth; 0.1 per cent owned one-third.'[36]
- From 1880–1909 the number of people who died leaving fortunes of over £2 million was 22; from 1910–39 this figure increased to 61.[37]
- Half a million acres of land were on sale in the summer of 1919, yet, in the interwar years, there were 'thirty landed millionaires and over seventy half-millionaires.'[38]
- Between 1911 and 1950, 420 new peerages were created, bringing into the aristocracy 'men of business, public service, and political background.'[39]

- In 1931, 524 out of 691 (76 per cent) holders of 'high office' in politics, business, the professions and administration had been educated at public school. The figure for 1942 was almost identical.[40]

There was one member of 'society' who drew more attention than any other during this period. In 1936 the dashing and popular Edward VIII decided to abdicate the throne in favour of his brother George VI, in order to marry the woman he loved, the American divorcee, Mrs Wallis Simpson. What do you think was the public reaction to this? What effects did it have on the standing of the monarchy?

4
THE BRITISH WAY OF LIFE
Education

Pupils in a Roman Catholic school being given a lecture on healthy eating in 1925. What differences are there between the school in the picture and one today?

THE PICTURE ABOVE is of a British elementary school between the wars. Although this school was not necessarily typical, what does the photograph suggest were the problems facing teachers, pupils and education authorities during this period?

For many years governments had recognized the need for the country to have a good education system, catering for the needs of all pupils. The greatest single drawback in putting this into practice, however, was lack of finance. Although government expenditure on education rose from £43.2 million in 1920 to £65.0 million in 1940, this still represented a tiny fraction of overall government spending, and much less than is spent on education today.[41] Although the school-leaving age had been raised to fourteen in 1918, by 1938 only about 74 per cent of children aged between twelve and fourteen were attending school. This was a rise of about 9 per cent from 1921. Almost three-quarters of all children were going to work by the age of fourteen, while for those a year older the figure was nearer 90 per cent.

Educational provision was based upon the 1870 Education Act, which established nation-wide state elementary education, and the 1902 Act which enabled state secondary schools ('county' schools) to be set up. Children could stay at their elementary school, learning little more than the 'three Rs', to the age of fourteen (the age fixed by the 1918 Education Act), or transfer to the county school at eleven, after an exam. For the majority of less well-off, the exams in English, arithmetic and general knowledge proved a tough hurdle, but those who passed received their secondary education free. For those who could afford fees of between three and five guineas (£3.15–£5.25) a term, entry was easier.

The 1918 Education Act and, more importantly, the government-accepted 1926 Hadlow Report recommended a universal system of national state education, from the age of five to the provision of university places, evening classes and technical training. Hadlow suggested primary education for all up to the age of eleven, after which children would progress to 'modern' or, for the more academic, 'grammar' schools. Many fine grammar schools were established, often providing the essential ladder up which a few talented students from poor backgrounds could move to university. One such pupil remembers:

> When, by a devious stroke of fortune, at the age of fourteen I was translated from my village elementary school to the ancient grammar school ten miles away, I entered a different world.[42]

In 1934, only 1 per cent of all students went on to university, and this small sector tended to be dominated, especially at the ancient universities of Oxford and Cambridge, by the privileged pupils who had had expensive private education. With their superior facilities, dedicated and talented staff, and small classes, the public schools ensured that between the wars the path to prosperity and influence remained vastly easier for the children of the wealthy than for the bulk of the population.

▲ Cambridge undergraduates, 1926. Only a tiny number of students were fortunate enough to receive a university education.

▼ The privileged few: pupils at Harrow School join in an ancient ritual on their Speech Day, 1932. Between the wars, ex-public school students continued to dominate society and government.

Sport

A historian of the inter-war period wrote:

Almost all sports but archery, bowls and croquet gained in popularity during this period, the greatest advances being in swimming and Association football.[43]

Why do you think this was the case? Part of the answer is contained in the next sentence from the same source:

Before the war, practically no lower- middle- or working-class people, except in sea-coast towns, could swim; now covered and open-air swimming baths, to which elementary school children were taken, and cheap excursions by road and rail to the sea made the non-swimmer feel behind the times.[44]

Sport was blossoming into the major industry it is today because most people had more leisure time and money, because transport was cheap, and because the nation was becoming aware that exercise was beneficial to the health.

As with so many other aspects of life between the wars, sport divided largely along class lines, although there were important points of contact, notably cricket.

For the majority of the population, whom we term the working class, football was the major winter sport. There were clubs and leagues up and down the country, with the first division sides regularly drawing huge crowds. When the first F.A. Cup Final was staged at the new Wembley Stadium in 1923, over 150,000 turned up to try to see the game. Football pools flourished, by 1938 10 million people invested £40 million in the hope of winning a fortune. Horse and greyhound racing (which started in Manchester in 1926), were the other gamblers' delights – in 1931, 18 million spectators 'went to the dogs'. Race horses, owned and trained by the wealthy but ridden and betted upon by ordinary people, were an important point of contact between the classes. Boxing, often rough and dangerous, was essentially a working-class sport, although it persisted in many public schools.

Football was the most popular spectator sport between the wars. Since there was no television, live matches, like this 1933 Wembley Cup Final, were always well attended.

THE THREAT
of losing a trim slender figure

HOW TO AVOID THAT FUTURE SHADOW

Ask your doctor! Over-weight is harmful. It makes for sluggish health and destroys the trim, slender figure of fashion. And over-weight is generally caused by eating between meals. So don't eat between meals. That's the time to **smoke a Kensitas** instead. Your desire will be pleasantly forgotten in the mellow satisfaction of the appetising aroma of Kensitas. Don't eat between meals, **smoke a Kensitas instead.**

MANUFACTURED BY THE
KENSITAS PRIVATE PROCESS

10 *for* 6ᵈ – 20 *for* 1/-

As good as really good cigarettes can be

"Your Kensitas Sir"
Cigarettes
REAL VIRGINIA

▲ This contemporary advertisement for Kensitas cigarettes shows how little people knew of the dangers of smoking.

Apart from South Wales, the Scottish borders and Cornwall, rugby football was a middle-class pursuit. So were golf and tennis, both of which enjoyed ever-mounting popularity. Cycling, motor cycling and hiking drew increasing numbers of enthusiasts from a variety of social groups. Motor sport, whether racing or rallying, was an extremely dangerous and expensive occupation for the well-to-do.

However, nothing seemed to typify the spirit of the nation between the wars more than cricket. The sport enjoyed a golden age. The names of the great batsmen, Hobbs, Sutcliffe, Hutton, or the demon bowlers, Larwood, Verity, Tate, were known in every household up and down the land. Yet a glance at a scorecard from the period shows how even on the cricket field the class divisions stood firm: professional players were known simply by their surnames; amateurs ('gentlemen') enjoyed the prefix 'Mr' – and changed in separate dressing rooms.

▼ Cricket was at the height of its popularity between the wars, but professional players were still looked down upon by amateurs.

The arts

The serious 'inter-war writers present a puzzle to the historian', notes A.J.P. Taylor.

> *Literature, according to historical convention, reflects contemporary life and reveals its spirit. To judge from all leading writers, the barbarians were breaking in. The decline and fall of the Roman empire were being repeated. Civilized men could only lament and withdraw . . . it is not easy to see why they thus cut themselves off . . . This was the best time mankind, or at any rate Englishmen, had known . . . It is hardly surprising that ordinary men and women found the great contemporary works of literature beyond them.*[45]

What do you think that Taylor means when he says that writers felt that 'the barbarians were breaking in'? Could it be that many writers and poets resented the fact that between the wars, with the expansion of education, together with greater leisure and affluence, culture was no longer the preserve of a tiny intellectual class but, increasingly, of everyone?

The 'difficult' writers to whom he refers are authors such as the Anglo-American

Jazz, such as that played by the Wolverine Orchestra shown in this picture, was the 'pop' music of the inter-war years. The older generation regarded it as decadent.

poet T.S. Eliot, Virginia Woolf and James Joyce, whose last work, *Finnegan's Wake*, although breaking new ground in the novel form, remained largely unintelligible. But the great mass of the reading public, fed by plentiful public libraries and the new six-penny (2½p) paperbacks, had plenty of other literature to read. There was political and social satire from George Orwell, Aldous Huxley and Evelyn Waugh. Graham Greene wrote some of the best novels of the period, W.H. Auden's poetry reflected the concerns of the 1930s, while for a lighter mood readers could turn to P.G. Wodehouse or Agatha Christie.

With a few notable exceptions, such as the painter Ben Nicholson, British painting and serious music were relatively conventional and uninspired. The two radical changes were the popularization of so-called 'classical' music through the gramophone and the BBC, and the influence of jazz, arriving from the USA in 1919 with the

Original Dixieland Jazz Band. British sculptors, however, were in the vanguard of their art form, led by Henry Moore, the American exile Jacob Epstein, Barbara Hepworth and the enigmatic Eric Gill.

It was not until after the Second World War that British theatre began a scintillating revival. The inter-war years were dominated by the well-made play, revivals, lighter revues and musical comedy. But for the masses the theatre was totally overshadowed by a new cultural medium, the cinema.

Although good seats at a cinema cost 2s 4d (11½p), for as little as 6d (2½p) a man or woman could leave the grey streets, at almost any time of day, for a softly-lit warm cocoon of pleasure. Here they could sit back, transported to a fantasy world of dashing heroes and seductive heroines.

▲ Charlie Chaplin, an English-born Hollywood actor, is shown here in the silent classic, *The Gold Rush* (1925).

▼ Between the wars every town had at least one cinema. Why do fewer people go to the pictures nowadays?

Entertainment

Between the wars the new but universally popular means of home entertainment was the radio. Traditional family pastimes, such as card-playing or singing round the piano, were swept aside. John Reith, the first Director-General of the BBC, announced:

> *The policy of the BBC . . . [is] to bring the best of everything into the greatest number of homes.*[46]

He believed that it was the duty of his organization to educate the masses.

Yet, despite Reith's high ideals, the BBC had its critics, from the 'respectable' gentleman who refused to let his daughter listen to 'love songs or dance music', the lady who demanded her license fee back because she had heard the word 'botheration' on Children's Hour, or the person who condemned 'the morons who . . . keep their wireless going all day' merely 'to gratify the passion for noise which is so characteristic of this singularly unaesthetic generation.'[47] What do these remarks tell you about middle-class attitudes of the time?

Reading was the other form of domestic entertainment expanding rapidly after the

UNDERGROUND

BOOK TO HAMPSTEAD OR GOLDERS GREEN

▲ London's underground railway system enabled millions of people to travel swiftly and cheaply at a time when private cars were still a luxury, even for the well-paid.

◀ A BBC radio newsreader, in 1932. It is said that the wireless, as it was then known, moulded the tastes and accents of several generations.

A crowded holiday beach in 1935. Why is it unusual today to find an English resort so full?

First World War. The circulation of daily newspapers rose from less than 4.5 million in 1910 to 10.5 million by 1939, while borrowings from public libraries went up to 207.9 million volumes in 1939, from 85.6 million in 1924. This, too, was the age of Billy Bunter and famous comics such as the *Boy's Own Paper*, the *Hotspur* and *Wizard*. Weekly papers for adults, especially women, also blossomed: *Home and Gardens* first appeared in 1919, *Woman's Own* in 1932 and *True Romances* in 1934. These were all products of a more leisured, affluent society.

Outside the home sport became big business, while the cinema gave millions a way of escape from the more unpleasant side of life:

Now I go to the pictures every week . . . Without films I am miserable. Sometimes I think they have become a habit, almost a drug.[48]

A crowded holiday beach in 1935. Why is it unusual today to find an English resort so full?

All the while, organized religion, dealt shattering blows by industrial urbanization, the growth of scientific thought, and the First World War, continued its decline towards the fragmented uncertainty we find in the latter half of the twentieth century. The pub also declined as a social centre for the community, as people drank less but smoked far more.

Although it was not until 1939 that the Holidays Act made a week's paid holiday a blessing to be enjoyed by most workers, the annual holiday had, for those in work, become a central feature of the inter-war years. Seaside resorts, such as Skegness and Blackpool, boomed, and Billy Butlin established his first holiday camp in 1937. By the 1930s over one million better-off holidaymakers were taking their annual break abroad.

5
BRITAIN AND THE WORLD
Shattered dreams 1919–39

THE GREATEST SINGLE problem confronting political historians is that they know how their story will end before they begin it. They are thus tempted to inflate the importance of facts that relate to the known future, and ignore happenings, however significant they might have seemed at the time, that had no long-term consequences. We know that attempts to preserve the peace of 1919 failed, so the temptation is to see them as bound to fail, and to wonder why more politicians did not heed the warnings of Winston Churchill, who predicted a second war with Germany long before it eventually came. Remarks like that of Marshal Foch, who in 1919 described the Treaty of Versailles as a 'twenty-year truce', are given exaggerated importance.

Four issues dominated British politics in 1918. One was how to cope with an increasingly restless and expensive empire. No satisfactory solution to the problem was found until after the Second World War, when gradually Britain's colonies were granted independence. In the meantime, the Imperial Conference of 1926 recognized Britain and its Dominions as independent states of equal status, while two India Acts (1919 and 1935) attempted to grant India, the largest and most troubled colony, a degree of self-government.

Ireland was a second problem. Civil war in 1919 resulted in the partition of the country in 1921 and the granting of dominion status to the south.

A third problem was Germany and its defeated allies. The solution was a series of remarkably harsh treaties, known collectively by that forced on Germany – the Treaty of Versailles – which broke up the defeated nations, limited their armaments and forced them to pay crippling reparations.

Winston Churchill was one of the few politicians who consistently warned against the build-up of Nazi power in the 1930s.

◄ German troops breaking the Treaty of Versailles by entering the Rhineland in 1936. The local inhabitants greeted the Nazis warmly.

▼ The Locarno conference, 1925, at which the Germans agreed voluntarily to the terms imposed upon them at the Treaty of Versailles seven years previously.

The final problem, the longest and most perplexing, was how to ensure that a major war never broke out again. The solution decided upon had three parts:
1 Restrictions on the aggressors of 1914, so that they could never make war. This was done in the peace treaties.
2 The formation of a League of Nations, to which all countries would eventually belong and which would foster international co-operation, as well as enforcing collective security by uniting against aggressors. Italy openly flouted the League in 1923 and 1935, Japan in 1931 and Germany repeatedly after 1933.
3 A series of international agreements on questions such as the frontiers of Germany (Locarno, 1925), naval limitations (Washington, 1922; London, 1930), and to ease war-like tension (Munich, 1938).

In the end these all failed. Amoral and powerful aggressors like Adolf Hitler were not bound by pieces of paper, but the well-intentioned statesmen who signed on Britain's behalf should not be too readily scorned for their misguided efforts.

The search for peace

Prime Minister Lloyd George argued the British point of view in the negotiations that led up to the 1919 Treaty of Versailles. He called for a reasonable, moderate settlement. Here are the main terms of the treaty; do you think they are in line with Lloyd George's way of thinking?

1 All German colonies were handed over to the League of Nations.

2 Much German territory was surrendered to other nations; for example Alsace-Lorraine to France. Germany and Austria were forbidden to unite.

3 The prosperous Saar coalfield was put under French control; the Rhineland was to be demilitarized.

4 Strict limitations were placed on German armed forces; for example the small army of 100,000 men was to have no tanks, while the navy could have no submarines.

5 Germany had to accept that it had caused the war and pay £6,600 million in reparations to the victorious allies.

In 1919 the economist J.M. Keynes wrote:

> . . . vengeance, I dare predict, will not limp . . . The horrors of the late German war will fade into nothing . . . in a new war which will inevitably arise if the economic terms forced on Germany are too harsh.[49]

The Europe created by the Treaty of Versailles, 1919.

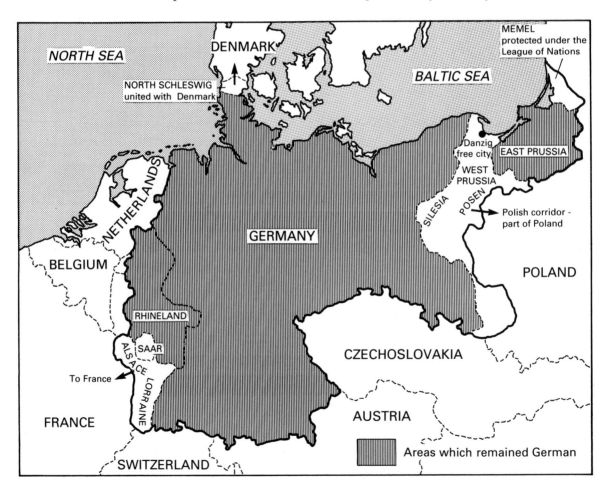

The British fleet being reviewed by the King in 1937. Economic cutbacks brought about as a result of the depression meant that the navy was in no fit state for world war at this time.

But during the 1920s such gloomy predictions seemed out of place. The League of Nations, which Britain supported whole-heartedly, managed to settle a number of minor disputes around the world and assisted post-war reconstruction by negotiating loans and helping refugees. This was despite the fact that neither the USA nor the USSR were League members. In 1924 the Labour government recognized the hitherto rather frightening new communist régime in the USSR.

A series of optimistic arms treaties also marked these years. The first came in 1922, when the USA, Britain, Japan, France and Italy agreed to limit the size of their navies in relation to each other. In 1928 Britain, along with 55 other governments, eventually signed the Kellogg-Briand Pact, officially renouncing war as a way of settling disputes. A further naval agreement was signed in 1930, and in 1932 Britain attended a massive disarmament conference in Geneva, seeking to find a way of bringing about universal world-wide disarmament.

Finally, at Locarno in 1925, Britain agreed to guarantee a series of treaties between France, Germany and Belgium which confirmed Germany's western frontiers as established in the Versailles treaties. Germany, which had its reparations repayments eased by the 1924 Dawes Plan, was now once more a fully-fledged member of the community of nations. In 1926 it joined the League.

So by the late 1920s the international scene looked set fair. With the USA and the USSR largely isolated from the mainstream of world politics, Britain could be seen to be as powerful and influential as ever. But upon what flimsy foundations did this peace and influence stand?

Ireland

POBLACHT NA H EIREANN.
THE PROVISIONAL GOVERNMENT
OF THE
IRISH REPUBLIC
TO THE PEOPLE OF IRELAND.

IRISHMEN AND IRISHWOMEN: In the name of God and of the dead generations from which she receives her old tradition of nationhood, Ireland, through us, summons her children to her flag and strikes for her freedom.

Having organised and trained her manhood through her secret revolutionary organisation, the Irish Republican Brotherhood, and through her open military organisations, the Irish Volunteers and the Irish Citizen Army, having patiently perfected her discipline, having resolutely waited for the right moment to reveal itself, she now seizes that moment, and, supported by her exiled children in America and by gallant allies in Europe, but relying in the first on her own strength, she strikes in full confidence of victory.

We declare the right of the people of Ireland to the ownership of Ireland, and to the unfettered control of Irish destinies, to be sovereign and indefeasible. The long usurpation of that right by a foreign people and government has not extinguished the right, nor can it ever be extinguished except by the destruction of the Irish people. In every generation the Irish people have asserted their right to national freedom and sovereignty; six times during the past three hundred years they have asserted it in arms. Standing on that fundamental right and again asserting it in arms in the face of the world, we hereby proclaim the Irish Republic as a Sovereign Independent State, and we pledge our lives and the lives of our comrades-in-arms to the cause of its freedom, of its welfare, and of its exaltation among the nations.

The Irish Republic is entitled to, and hereby claims, the allegiance of every Irishman and Irishwoman. The Republic guarantees religious and civil liberty, equal rights and equal opportunities to all its citizens, and declares its resolve to pursue the happiness and prosperity of the whole nation and of all its parts, cherishing all the children of the nation equally, and oblivious of the differences carefully fostered by an alien government, which have divided a minority from the majority in the past.

Until our arms have brought the opportune moment for the establishment of a permanent National Government, representative of the whole people of Ireland and elected by the suffrages of all her men and women, the Provisional Government, hereby constituted, will administer the civil and military affairs of the Republic in trust for the people.

We place the cause of the Irish Republic under the protection of the Most High God, Whose blessing we invoke upon our arms, and we pray that no one who serves that cause will dishonour it by cowardice, inhumanity, or rapine. In this supreme hour the Irish nation must, by its valour and discipline and by the readiness of its children to sacrifice themselves for the common good, prove itself worthy of the august destiny to which it is called.

Signed on Behalf of the Provisional Government,
THOMAS J. CLARKE,
SEAN Mac DIARMADA, THOMAS Mac DONAGH,
P. H. PEARSE, EAMONN CEANNT,
JAMES CONNOLLY. JOSEPH PLUNKETT.

This declaration was read out in Dublin at Easter 1916 to mark the start of a rising against Britain, which ruled all of Ireland at that time. What was the significance of the word 'republic'?

The Liberal prime minister, Asquith, referred to the problem of Ireland as 'The Damnable Question'. His reasons for doing so were straightforward. For centuries British politicians had tried to settle an issue which seemed beyond settlement. Unwilling to leave a potentially hostile independent Roman Catholic state on their western flank, in the sixteenth and seventeenth centuries the British had conquered Ireland and settled many Protestants there, largely in the north.

In 1800 an Act of Union merged Ireland with the rest of Britain, to form the United Kingdom of Great Britain and Ireland. Over the next century a powerful independence movement grew up among the Irish, which after 1885 the Liberal Party supported. In 1912 an Irish Home Rule Bill was passed by the House of Commons and was due to come into effect in 1914. But the Protestant 'Unionists' in the north (an area often known simply as 'Ulster'), wished to remain part of the United Kingdom, and rejected Home Rule. In this they were supported by the Conservatives. So in 1914 Ireland was on the point of civil war.

With the outbreak of the First World War, Home Rule was shelved. This enraged many Irish, and on Easter Sunday 1916 rebels seized the centre of Dublin, declaring a republic. The Easter Rising, as it became known, was brutally suppressed by British troops, which greatly increased the resentment felt towards the British.

The Ulster Unionists had demonstrated their loyalty in blood, on the battlefields of the First World War:

> On 1 July the battle of the Somme opened, and the 36th (Ulster) Division was ordered out of their section of the British lines . . . to attack the German lines. They attacked with tremendous courage . . . and in two days of battle . . . ended more or less where they had begun, in terms of ground gained. But their dead were heaped in thousands on the German wire and littered the ground . . . half of Ulster was in mourning.[50]

A very young boy prepares to throw a petrol bomb, during disturbances in Northern Ireland. The solution Britain imposed in the 1920s, to divide Ireland, left many dissatisfied, and lies behind the troubles that continue to this day.

Why do you think that the slaughter on the Somme and the bloody quelling of the Easter Rising made a future settlement in Ireland even more difficult to achieve?

With the war over, by 1919 Ireland was consumed by Civil War between the Irish Republican Army (IRA) and British forces, known from their uniform as the 'Black and Tans'. Lloyd George's government now had to accept the inevitable. A Government of Ireland Act split the country between the North, which remained in the United Kingdom, and the South, which in 1932 became the fully independent state of Eire. Fighting continued in the South until 1923, as there were many 'Republicans' who refused to accept the division of the country.

A settlement had been imposed which no group found wholly acceptable. Can you see within the settlement the seeds of the troubles which, breaking out afresh in the late 1960s, continue into the latter half of the twentieth century?

Appeasement

This map shows the spread of German power. Hitler's aim was to regain land lost by the Treaty of Versailles, and to gain *lebensraum* (living space).

There are, in simple terms, two ways of preserving peace. One is to ensure that a country is so powerful that no enemy dare attack, and any sign of hostility can be crushed before it becomes too threatening. The second is to negotiate with aggressors in the belief that they will listen to reason, and that discussion is always preferable to war. During the late 1930s the British government followed this second course, a policy which became known as appeasement.

The collapse of international order, which eventually led to the Second World War, began with the Wall Street Crash of 1929 and the world-wide economic depression which followed it. In keeping with many other nations, Britain cut its expenditure on defence and tried, at the League of Nations

Disarmament Conference (1932–1934), to get all countries to reduce their armaments. However, in Japan and Germany nationalist governments came to power, promising their impoverished followers glory through foreign conquest.

During the 1930s, successive acts of international aggression by Japan, Germany and Italy went unchecked. Japan's invasion of Manchuria in 1931, Nazi Germany's annexation of Austria in 1938, and Mussolini's invasion of Abyssinia in 1935 all signalled the failure of the League of Nations. The newly-allied fascist dictators, Hitler and Mussolini, used the Spanish Civil War (1936–9) as a testing ground for their modern armaments and to flex their military muscle before the world.

At first the British government was unsure how to treat fascism. A generous Naval Treaty was made with Germany in 1935, and at Munich in 1938 Prime Minister Chamberlain agreed to Hitler's seizure of western Czechoslovakia. But when, in the spring of 1939, Hitler broke this agreement and took the rest of Czechoslovakia, Chamberlain realized that Hitler was not to be trusted.

The final blow came in August 1939 when Germany made a cynical Non-Aggression Pact with its bitterest enemy, the USSR, and launched an invasion of Poland less than a month later. Britain and France now had no choice but to declare war on Germany. Appeasement had failed.

Five arguments in support of appeasement can be put forward:

1 Britain was not ready for war – in 1936 arms expenditure was less than half that of Germany. The British air force was inadequate. There was no way Britain could have interfered effectively in Eastern Europe, Abyssinia or China. Time to re-arm was essential – appeasement bought this time.

2 Hitler would not have risked war in the west with a hostile USSR in the east.

3 The British people did not want war. In March 1938 only 33 per cent of people believed that Britain should intervene to help Czechoslovakia.[51]

4 The Treaty of Versailles had been unjust. Britain had no right to dictate any further to the German people.

5 Aerial attack, perhaps with gas bombs, made modern warfare so terrible that it should be avoided at all costs.

These are strong arguments. Do you think that Chamberlain could reasonably have been expected to follow any policy other than appeasement?

Many British politicians failed to take Hitler seriously until it was too late. They had some respect for the way he improved the German economy and turned a blind eye to his more sinister exploits.

The long weekend

WE LIVE IN AN AGE of symbols and images. Advertising and the media strive to encapsulate complex issues in a well-chosen phrase or memorable picture. The inter-war years have suffered from this desire to simplify, for the images from that era which most readily stick in our minds do not tell the full story.

In 1938 Neville Chamberlain returned from his famous meeting with Hitler at Munich declaring of his settlement: 'I believe it is peace for our time.'[52] The comment turned out to be one of history's cruellest jokes. Less than a year later Britain was at war. The embittered politician confessed to Parliament:

> . . . everything that I have worked for, everything that I have hoped for, everything that I have believed in during my public life, has crashed in ruins.[53]

A cloud of failure hangs over these years.

The picture of gloom is reinforced by other memorable but depressing features of the time: the General Strike, the Jarrow March, massive unemployment, the so-called betrayal of his party by the Labour prime minister Ramsay MacDonald in 1931, the ineffective bullying of the British Raj when faced with the moral arguments of Mohatma Gandhi. If we accept these as signs of the age, it is little wonder that the period has been called the 'Long Weekend' – a time when little was achieved, when Britain rested, willingly or unwillingly.

But this is to distort the truth. In fact, the true watershed of modern history was the First World War. It changed Britain radically and permanently, in a way that the war of 1939–45 was never to do. There is a real continuity from 1919 to the present day. The inter-war years witnessed the creation of our present-day world.

We can now see that the lasting features of this period were not those that

The famous Jarrow Hunger March, which captured the popular imagination, has left us with a vivid image of the inter-war years as grim and poverty-stricken.

immediately caught the eye. What has endured from that time is the leisured consumer society: homes served by electricity, motor cars, radio and television; holidays; Labour governments; women's rights; widespread birth-control; an interest in sport; government welfare; expanding education; and lively, popular music. 'In this England,' wrote J.B. Priestley in 1934:

> . . . for the first time in their history, Jack and Jill are nearly as good as their master and mistress . . . [Britain] is a cleaner, tidier, healthier, saner world than that of nineteenth century industrialism.[54]

Bank holiday crowds at Waterloo station, 1938. For those in employment, Britain was a country of rising prosperity and improving living standards.

Yet there was no golden age. The high hopes of 1919 that the country would become, in Lloyd George's words, a country 'fit for heroes to live in', soon faded. There are many alive today who still regard the inter-war years with gloom, for we have moved on to a time of greater prosperity and opportunity. Nevertheless, although the greatest single aim - to preserve the peace that had been so hard-won – was not fulfilled, the inter-war years were a time when the majority of British citizens could view the future with reasonable optimism.

Leading figures

W.M. Aitken, Lord Beaverbrook (1879–1964) newspaper owner

The son of a Canadian Presbyterian minister, Aitken made a fortune before emigrating to Britain in 1910. After being an MP, he built up a massive newspaper empire, acquiring the *Daily Express* (1917), the *Sunday Express* (1921), and the *Evening Standard* (1929). In his hands the *Express* became the newspaper with the world's largest circulation. Beaverbrook used his papers to put forward his strong prejudices in favour of the British Empire and Winston Churchill, but bitterly hostile to Baldwin and Nazi Germany. When Churchill became prime minister in 1940 he rewarded Lord Beaverbrook with the post of Minister of Aircraft Production.

Nancy W. Astor (1879–1964) politician and feminist

Nancy Astor was born in the USA and married into a well-known family of American millionaires. Upon settling in Britain she became famous as the first woman MP to take her seat in the House of Commons. (Countess Markiewicz was the first woman elected to Parliament, but as she was a member of the Irish nationalist party, Sinn Fein, she did not go to Westminster.) Nancy Astor was Conservative MP for Plymouth until 1945. A well-known political hostess, she exercised influence on Conservative policy, as well as campaigning effectively for education, temperance and women's rights.

Lord Beaverbrook, seated at his desk.

Herbert Austin (1866–1941) motor manufacturer

After gaining experience as an engineer in Australia, Herbert Austin returned to Britain and became one of the first men to realize the potential of a petrol-driven motor car. By 1914 he had built up a sizeable business at Longbridge outside Birmingham, but his real success came with the 'baby' Austin 7 of 1922. Although William Morris was the first to mass-produce cars in Britain, Austin's new cheap, small but reliable vehicle for the first time brought motoring within the range of the ordinary middle-class family.

Stanley Baldwin (1867–1947) Conservative politician

Born into a successful business family, Baldwin received a traditional English upper-class education (Harrow and Cambridge) before beginning his political career

Herbert Austin, demonstrating one of his cars.

in 1908. Working his way up the Conservative Party ladder, he was chosen, amid great controversy, as prime minister in 1923. With breaks in 1924 and 1929–35, he retained the premiership until 1937, stepping down after successfully handling the crisis surrounding the abdication of Edward VIII. Although he has been criticized for mishandling the questions of unemployment and re-armament, Baldwin was an effective politician, whose leadership held his party together and gave the nation a sense of security and unity during difficult times.

A. Neville Chamberlain (1868–1940) Conservative politician

Neville Chamberlain, whose father was a leading politician of late Victorian and Edwardian times, first became an MP in

1918. He held several government posts, twice being Chancellor of the Exchequer (1923–4 and 1931–7), before serving as prime minister (1937–40). A cautious and painstaking man, he is best remembered for stubbornly adhering to a policy of appeasement in the face of Nazi aggression. Recently historians have become increasingly critical of his handling of international affairs in the years leading up to the outbreak of war in September 1939.

Charlie Chaplin (1889–1977) actor and producer

Charlie Chaplin is probably the best-remembered figure from the inter-war years. Although his Chaplin Studios were based in Hollywood, USA, his work owed much to his London background and was always hugely popular in Britain. His most famous role was as the unfortunate, bowler-hatted tramp, pathetically in love, usually knocked about by the arrogant and wealthy. Chaplin's wistfully amusing work also contained sharp comment on the false values of society, notable in films such as *Modern Times* (1936). Chaplin became increasingly socialist in his convictions, leading him to make a striking attack on the Nazis in *The Great Dictator* (1940).

Winston S. Churchill (1874–1965) statesman

At the end of the First World War Winston Churchill, who already had a major political reputation, was Liberal Minister of Munitions. He was Chancellor of the Exchequer from 1924 to 1929, when he returned Britain to the Gold Standard. He attracted attention for the way he handled the information services during the 1926 General Strike. Opposed to giving concessions to the Indian nationalists and to Hitler's Nazis, he remained out of office throughout the 1930s. Many of his warnings about the rise of German power proved prophetic and he was called upon to serve as prime minister in 1940.

D.H. Lawrence (1885–1930) writer

Many would claim that D.H. Lawrence is one of the greatest British novelists of the twentieth century, although critics point to his lack of humour and an obsession with sex which appears almost ridiculous to more liberated generations. The son of a Nottinghamshire miner, he wrote his partly autobiographical work, *Sons and Lovers*, in 1913. Between the wars he left England and wrote many fine novels, including *The Rainbow*, (1915), *Women in Love* (1920) and *Lady Chatterley's Lover* (1928). This last work was banned in Britain until 1960 for its frank handling of sexual passion which included the use of obscene words.

David Lloyd George (1863–1945) Liberal politician

Although most of Lloyd George's achievements occurred before 1918, he was one of the most able politicians of the inter-war years. As prime minister of a coalition government between 1918 and 1922, he was responsible for heading the British delegation at the Versailles peace conference, where he exercised a moderating influence, and for temporarily settling the vexed problem of Ireland with the 1920 Government of Ireland Act. Rejected by the Tories in 1922, he remained leader of the Liberal Party until 1926, after which he sat in the Commons as an independent Liberal until shortly before his death.

J. Ramsay MacDonald (1866–1937) Labour politician

From a very poor Scottish background, Ramsay MacDonald rose to become secretary of the Labour Representation Committee in 1900 and of the Labour Party in 1906. With a short break from 1918–22, when his pacifist principles led to his rejection, between 1906 and 1937 he represented several constituencies in the House of Commons.

He was prime minister and foreign secretary in the first Labour government (1924), then prime minister in the second Labour ministry (1929–31), and in the National Government between 1931 and 1935. Although he was accused of splitting the Labour Party in 1931, he did more than any other politician to earn for his party the responsible and trustworthy image that many of the electorate found reassuring.

J.C.W. Reith (1889–1971) Director-General of the BBC

John Reith (later Lord Reith) had as much influence on inter-war Britain as any politician. In 1922 he became General Manager of the British Broadcasting Company (BBC), later serving as Director-General of the Corporation, 1927–38. A tough and ruthless Calvinist, he believed that the task of the BBC was not just to entertain but to educate the nation. He insisted on the highest – sometimes ridiculous – standards: radio newsreaders, for example, were required to wear dinner jackets when in front of the microphone. Nevertheless, he did much to create for the BBC its world-wide reputation for integrity, even-handedness and technical competence.

Marie Stopes (1880–1958) doctor and feminist

Dr Stopes trained in London and Munich before becoming the first woman lecturer at Manchester University. She worked in Japan, and on returning to England married the aircraft pioneer H.V. Roe, with whose backing she was able to found the first British birth-control clinic. She had already made a name for herself with *Married Love* (1918), a book which made widely available details of contraceptive techniques. Although she received condemnation for her outspoken treatment of a 'taboo' subject, her work marked an important step in the 'sexual revolution' which has been a major feature of our century.

Marie Stopes, who founded the first birth-control clinic.

Important dates

Dates	Events

Dates   Events

1918   Representation of the People Act gives the vote to women over thirty.
Armistice ends the First World War.
Education Act.
General election: majority for Lloyd George's coalition government.

1919   Peace talks at Versailles; treaty comes into force the following year.
Troubles in Ireland.
Viscountess Astor is the first woman MP to take her seat in the Commons.

1920   Civil War in Ireland.

1921   Trade agreement with the USSR.
Miners' strike.
Dominion status for Southern Ireland.

1922   Conservatives reject Lloyd George and form government under Bonar Law.
BBC begins broadcasting.
General election: Conservative victory.

1923   Baldwin becomes prime minister.
General election: no single party with overall majority; Baldwin remains prime minister.

1924   First Labour government, under Ramsay MacDonald, lasts January–October. Baldwin forms
Conservative government after election victory.
Britain formally recognizes the USSR.

1925   Contributory state pensions introduced for all over 65.
Locarno treaties signed in London.

1926   General Strike.
Dominions given status equal to Britain in the empire.
Hadlow Report on education.

1927   General strikes made illegal.
Unemployment benefit cut.

1928   Voting age of women reduced to twenty-one.

1929   County councils made responsible for the poor.
General election: minority Labour government formed under MacDonald.
New York stock exchange crashes (Wall Street Crash).

1930   London Naval treaty.
Massive rise in unemployment.

1931   National Government formed under MacDonald – Labour Party split.
Japan invades Manchuria.
Strict government economy measures. Unemployment benefit subject to 'means' test.
General election: victory for National Government.

1932   Geneva disarmament conference begins.
Heavy import duties imposed.
Anglo-French pact of friendship.

1933   Hitler becomes Chancellor of Germany.
Large programme of slum clearance begins.

1935   Stresa Front formed between Britain, France and Italy.
Baldwin replaces MacDonald as prime minister.
Government of India Act.
General election: victory for National Government.

Dates   Events

1936   Spanish Civil War (to 1939).
        Mussolini invades Abyssinia.
        Abdication of Edward VIII.
        Education Act.
        Germany re-occupies Rhineland.
        Regular television broadcasts begin.
        'Jarrow crusade' march of unemployed from Jarrow to London.
1937   Chamberlain replaces Baldwin as prime minister.
        Anglo-German naval agreement.
        Germany annexes Austria.
        Factory Act.
1938   Munich agreement permits Hitler to take western Czechoslovakia.
1939   Germans overrun rest of Czechoslovakia.
        Nazi-Soviet Non-Aggression Pact.
        Second World War begins as Germans attack Poland.

Glossary

Abdicate	To give up the throne, or another responsibility.
Abyssinia	The name for Ethiopia before it gained independence.
Alliance	A bond or treaty made between countries to further their common interests.
Annex	To take over.
Antagonism	Hostility.
Appeasement	A policy of negotiation and compromise rather than confrontation.
Aristocracy	The titled upper class.
Armistice	Cease-fire.
Cabinet	Group of senior policy-making ministers of a government.
Capitalism	An economic theory that believes in the virtue of free enterprise, and the right to individual property and wealth.
Civil servant	Member of the administrative service of a government.
Coalition	A government where power is shared between more than one political party.
Colony	Overseas territory administered by another country.
Commercial	Relating to economic needs; having profit as the main aim.
Communism	A political and economic theory following the ideas of Karl Marx, who believed in the abolition of all private property and the creation of a classless society.
Compromise	To settle a dispute by finding a solution that satisfies all sides.
Conscription	Compulsory military service.
Cyclical	Moving in waves or cycles.
Decade	Ten years.
Demilitarize	Remove all troops and military installations.
Democracy	Rule by the people or their elected representatives.
Disarmament	Getting rid of (all) military weapons.
Dole	State unemployment benefit.
Dominion	An independent, equal, self-governing territory within the British Empire.
Duties	Taxes.
Economy	A country's finances, trade and industry.
Electorate	Those entitled to vote.
Elite	The top group, the best.
Emancipation	Setting free.
Empire	Widespread territories and peoples under one government.
Entrepreneur	A person who launches his or her own business.
Fabians	Early British socialists.
Flout	Openly to go against something.
Fragmented	Broken into pieces or sections.
Free trade	International trade based upon exchange of goods without customs duties.
Guinea	One pound and one shilling.
Hung parliament	One in which no party has an overall majority.

58

Imperialism	Policy of making or maintaining an empire.
Inflation	When money loses its value and prices rise faster than incomes.
Isolation	Being cut off; policy of avoiding political links with other countries.
Liberalism	A philosophy that advocates the freedom of the individual, and favours progress and reform.
Peerage	Those entitled to sit in the House of Lords.
Protection	Protecting domestic industry with high tariffs on imports.
Reparations	Compensation in money or materials paid by a defeated country to the victor.
Republic	A state governed without a king or queen.
Revenue	Government income.
Shilling	Part of the British currency before decimalization in 1971. 1/20 of £, divided into twelve old pennies.
Slump	Sudden economic collapse.
Socialism	An economic theory that believes that the state should own all important means of the production and distribution of wealth.
Statesman	An influential and internationally respected politician.
Stockbrokers	Those who deal in stocks and shares.
Stock exchange	The place where stocks and shares are bought and sold.
Tariff	Tax on goods entering or leaving a country.
'Three Rs'	Reading, Writing and Arithmetic.
Tory	Conservative.
Treaty	A written agreement between nations.
Urbanization	To make into a town or city; to modernize, and make less rural.
White-collar workers	Non-manual workers, e.g. office workers.

Further reading

General reading

Brown, R. and Daniels, C., *Twentieth Century Britain*, Macmillan, 1982.
Lloyd, I.O., *Empire to Welfare State: English History 1906–1976*, Oxford, 1979.
Robbins, K.G., *The Eclipse of a Great Power: Modern Britain 1870–1975*, Longman, 1983.
Taylor, A.J.P., *English History, 1914–1945*, Oxford, 1965.

Original sources

Brittain, V., *Testament of Youth*, Virago-Fontana, 1974.
Churchill, W.S., *The Gathering Storm*, Penguin, 1960.
Graves, R. and Hodge, A., *The Long Week-End: A Social History of Britain, 1918–1939*, Faber & Faber, 1940.
Orwell, G. *Down and Out in Paris and London*, Penguin, 1940.
Orwell, G., *The Road to Wigan Pier*, Penguin, 1941.
Priestley, J.B., *English Journey*, Heinemann, 1933.

Political

Adelman, P., *The Rise of the Labour Party 1880–1945*, Longman, 1972.
Blake, R., *The Conservative Party from Peel to Churchill*, Fontana, 1972.
Butler, D. and G., *British Political Facts, 1900–1985*, 6th edition, London, 1986.
Cook, C., *A Short History of the Liberal Party 1900–1976*, Macmillan, 1976.
Morris, M., *The General Strike*, Penguin, 1976.
Pelling, H., *A History of British Trade Unionism*, Penguin, 1963.
Pelling H., *Winston Churchill*, Macmillan, 1974.
Pugh, M., *The Making of Modern British Politics 1867–1939*, Blackwell, 1982.

Social and Economic

Constantine, S., *Unemployment in Britain Between the Wars*, Longman, 1980.
Gilbert, B.B., *British Social Policy 1914–1939*, Batsford, 1970.
Glynn, S. and Oxborrow, J., *Interwar Britain: A Social and Economic History*, Allen & Unwin, 1976.
Royle, E., *Modern Britain A Social History 1750–1985*, London, 1987.
Seaman, L.C.B., *Life in Britain Between the Wars*, Batsford, 1985.
Stevenson, J., *British Society 1914–1945*, Penguin, 1984.

Foreign Policy and Ireland

Adamthwaite, A. (ed.), *The Making of the Second World War*, Allen & Unwin, 1977.
Gilbert, M., *The Roots of Appeasement*, Weidenfeld & Nicholson, 1966.
Lyons, F.S.L., *Ireland Since the Famine*, Fontana, 1974.

Picture acknowledgements

The author and publisher would like to thank the following for allowing their illustrations to be reproduced in this book: Camera Press Ltd 9, 11 (right), 20, 26, 33, 36, 43 (both); the Centre for the Study of Cartoons and Caricature, University of Kent at Canterbury 10 (Bernard Partridge, *Punch*), 19 (L. Raven-Hill, *Punch*), 27 (Strube, *Daily Express*), 28 (Strube, *Daily Express*); Hulton Picture Company 5 (left), 6, 15 (both), 17, 21 (bottom), 29 (both), 30, 34, 37 (bottom); Topham Picture Library 4, 5 (right), 7 (both), 8, 11 (bottom), 12, 13, 16, 18, 19 (bottom), 21 (top), 22, 23 (both), 24, 25 (both), 31, 32, 35 (both), 38, 39 (both), 40 (bottom), 41, 42, 45, 46, 49, 50, 51. All other pictures are from the Wayland Picture Library. The artwork on pages 14, 44 and 48 was supplied by Peter Bull.

Notes on sources

1 Cited in Mowat, C.L., *Britain Between the Wars*, Methuen, 1956, p. 1.
2 Graves, R. and Hodge, A., *The Long Week-End*, Faber & Faber, 1940, p. 17.
3 Taylor, A.J.P., *English History 1914–1945*, Oxford, 1965, p. 129.
4 Cited in Briggs, A., *They Saw It Happen 1897–1940*, Blackwell, 1960, p. 393.
5 H. Macmillan, *The Middle Way*, 1938, pp. 173–4.
6 *English History 1914–1945*, Oxford, 1965, p. 209.
7 Cole, M. (ed.), *Beatrice Webb's Diaries*, Longman, 1952, p. 258.
8 Wilson, T., *The Downfall of the Liberal Party, 1914–1935*, Fontana, 1968, p. 421.
9 All these figures are from Cook, L. and Stevenson, J., *The Longman Handbook of Modern History 1714–1987*, Longman, 1988, pp. 189–222.
10 Stevenson, J., *British Society 1914–45*, Penguin, 1984, p. 103.
11 *Ibid.*, p. 273.
12 From Walter Greenwood's novel *Love On the Dole*, 1933, cited in Constantine, S., *Unemployment in Britain Between the Wars*, Longman, 1980, p. 85.
13 *English History 1914–1945*, *op. cit.*, chapter VII.
14 *Ibid.*, p. 260.
15 *The Long Week-End*, *op. cit.*; MacNiece's poem is cited in L.C.B. Seaman, *Life in Britain Between the Wars*, Batsford, 1985, p. 198.
16 Stevenson, *op. cit.*, p. 109.
17 *Ibid.*, pp. 110–112.
18 *Ibid.*, pp. 121–123.
19 *Ibid.*, p. 130 and Seaman *op. cit.*, pp. 131–2.
20 All the information in this paragraph comes from Halsey, A.H. (ed.), *Trends in British Society Since 1900*, Macmillan, 1972.
21 Stevenson, *op. cit.*, pp. 330–331.
22 'The English People' in *Collected Essays,*
Journalism and Letters of George Orwell, 4 vols., Penguin, 1970, Vol. 3, 1943–1945, p. 19.
23 Constantine, *op. cit.*, p. 4.
24 Cited in Seaman, *op. cit.*, pp. 34–5.
25 Halsey, *op. cit.*, p. 303.
26 *Ibid.*, p. 312.
27 Pelling, H., *A History of British Trade Unionism*, Penguin, 1969, pp. 261–264.
28 *Ibid.*
29 Stevenson, *op. cit.*, p. 180.
30 *Ibid.*, p. 150.
31 Cook and Stevenson, *op. cit.*, p. 155.
32 Cited in Barker, T. (ed.), *The Long March of Everyman*, Andre Deutsch, 1975, p. 225.
33 Cited in Stevenson, *op. cit.*, pp. 332–3.
34 *Op. cit.*, pp. 65–6.
35 *Op. cit.*, p. 204
36 A.J.P. Taylor, *op. cit.*, p. 171.
37 Stevenson, *op. cit.*, p. 331.
38 *Ibid.*, pp. 332 and 335.
39 *Ibid.*, p. 349.
40 *Ibid.*, p. 352.
41 Cook and Stevenson, *op. cit.*, p. 119.
42 Cited in Stevenson, *op. cit.*, p. 255.
43 Graves and Hodge, *op. cit.*, p. 232.
44 *Ibid.*
45 *Op. cit.*, p. 180.
46 Cited in Barker, T. (ed.), *op. cit.*, p. 238.
47 *Ibid.*, p. 239.
48 Cited in *ibid.*, p. 237.
49 *The Economic Consequences of the Peace*, Macmillan, 1924, p. 251.
50 From Liam de Paor, *Divided Ulster*, Penguin, 1971. Cited in Brown, R. and Daniels, C., *Twentieth Century Britain*, Macmillan, 1982, p. 32.
51 Cited in Shephard, K., *International Relations 1919–1939*, Blackwell, 1987, p. 45.
52 Cited, *inter alia*, in Mowat, *op. cit.*, p. 619.
53 *Ibid.*, p. 650.
54 Priestley, J.B., *English Journey*, Heinemann, 1934, p. 410.

Index

Figures in **bold** refer to illustrations.